Teen People

LOVE
stories

Other *Teen People* books:

Real Life Diaries
Sex Files

Teen People®

LOVE
stories

STORIES OF TRUE ROMANCE

Edited by Jennifer Soong

AVON BOOKS
An Imprint of HarperCollinsPublishers

Photo Credits

Permission to use the following photographs is gratefully acknowledged:
pages 2, 4, 6, 9, courtesy of Emily Johnson; page 12, courtesy of Kristi Piel;
pages 18, 21, 22, 24, courtesy of Gilbert Ayala; pages 28, 30, 32, 34–35,
courtesy of Renée Krajcik; pages 38, 42, courtesy of Robin Godfrey; page 46,
© Nick Farrell; page 50, courtesy of Catherine Nguyen; pages 52, 56,
© Gabrielle Revere; page 62, courtesy of Ingmar Erler; pages 65, 68, 72,
courtesy of Feather Rogers-Dayton; pages 74, 78, 83, courtesy of Jamie
Dwyer; pages 86, 90, 92, courtesy of Terese Opiela; pages 94, 97, 99, 101,
102, courtesy of Maria Alejandra Navas; page 106, © Jeaneen Lund; page 110,
© Keri Pickett; page 114, © Jeaneen Lund; page 118, © Emily Wilson.

Love Stories: Stories of True Romance
Copyright © 2001 by Time Inc.
Catherine Nguyen & Sinh Luong story (pages 47–51) was originally published
in *Teen People*, September 2000 issue.
Ann-Margaret Brannon & John Swearingen story (pages 53–59) was originally
published in *Teen People*, February 2001 issue.
Chapter 6: Reel-Life Romances was originally published in *Teen People*,
February 2001 issue.

Library of Congress Catalog Card Number: 2001116857
ISBN 0-06-447320-1
First Avon edition, 2001

AVON TRADEMARK REG. U.S. PAT. OFF. AND IN OTHER COUNTRIES,
MARCA REGISTRADA, HECHO EN U.S.A.

Visit us on the World Wide Web!
www.harperteen.com
www.teenpeople.com
AOL Keyword: Teen People

To all the teens who have shared
their stories with us.

Contents

Letter from the Editor

When I was fifteen, a guy in high school wanted to ask me out on a date, but my parents insisted on meeting him first. On the day he was supposed to come, we waited and waited. Finally I realized he wasn't going to show up.

I saw him at school the next day, and he told me he'd gotten lost. He didn't ask if we could reschedule the meeting with my parents. I felt hurt, embarrassed. I really liked him, and I took it personally.

Only years later did I realize how difficult it must have been for him to approach my neighborhood of big houses and manicured lawns. He was African-American, and I believe his fear of my parents and the recognition of our different lives is what really kept him away.

Everybody has a love story—or in my case, an unrequited love story. As the couples in *Teen People: Love Stories* show, a relationship often has to overcome a lot of obstacles before it can become a romance. Reading the story of Jamie Dwyer and Jamah Perry, two teens who overcame their different racial backgrounds to be together, reminded me of what I went through. But these are different times, and Jamie and Jamah dealt head-on with an issue that I hardly understood years ago.

Your teenage years are usually when your first significant romantic relationship happens, and it doesn't always go smoothly. The roadblocks can be small: misunderstandings over money or a casual flirtation. Or huge, as in the case of Ann-Margaret Brannon and John Swearingen, whose love thrives despite the fact that John is battling cancer. Some of these stories are about the magic of instant chemistry and the more subtle rewards of friendships that evolve into something more. Above all, *Love Stories* proves that the power of love can help you through difficult times and complicated situations.

I hope they inspire you to write your own love story. So don't sit by the phone waiting for someone to call. Read this book and make the call yourself.

Barbara O'Dair
Managing Editor, *Teen People*

Teen People

LOVE
stories

Chapter 1

friends
FIRST

These couples started as friends,
but soon discovered something more—love.

Emily Johnson, 19

Josh Peck, 17

DUVALL, WASHINGTON

Emily knew that Josh was the right guy for her even before they met in person. She got a positive vibe simply from seeing his photo at her friend's house. "I don't know why, but I thought he looked like someone who could be my best friend," she says. When she found out that he was going to an upcoming Halloween party, she was determined to find out if there was more to her feeling.

The night of the party, Emily made an entrance that caught everyone's attention, though it was definitely not by design. As she was walking down the stairs, she lost her balance, tripped on the steps and slid all the way to the bottom—landing right at Josh's feet. Turning a deep shade of crimson, Emily thought she

From the moment Emily and Josh met, something clicked.

had blown her chance with him. But Josh was unfazed, and smoothed everything out; he helped her up, gave her a hug and introduced himself. "From that very second, I knew that we were meant to be," she says. "Love was not on my mind yet. I just knew that I had never felt such a strong connection to anyone before."

As soon as they started chatting, the two felt completely at ease and talked as if they had known each other their entire lives. "By the end of the night, it was pretty flirtatious," recalls Josh. "Everybody was noticing, and after she left, all the guys were coming up to me to see if I asked her out yet."

Josh wanted to get to know her better first. He suggested Emily and their friends go to the movies, so they went to see *The Waterboy*. Even though it wasn't an official date, something clicked. "We held hands and it was just so wonderful," says Emily. "Usually when you like someone, you don't know if it'll work. But after we held hands, it was kind of inevitable that something was going to happen."

Perfect Timing

On Christmas, Josh planned to ask Emily to be his girlfriend. "I was thinking long and hard if I was ready to make the commitment," he explains. "And I decided I wanted to. It felt right." He called

Emily says, "I like him because . . . he's not one of those big tough guys who like football and cars."

her up and, pumped up on nervous energy, blurted out, "Would you like to go out sometime?" She thought he just wanted to hang out, and responded, "Where?" He was thrown off by her reaction, but he repeated his question. She still acted confused. After a moment's hesitation—and wondering if he should change his tack—he asked her a third time. "Right after that, I realized what he was doing," she recalls. "Then I got all nervous. But I said yes."

Emily says that Josh is different from most guys she knows. "I like him because he's funny and cute," she says. "He's not one of those big tough guys who like football and cars." Josh says, "I wasn't really brought up like that. My mom had her own ballet school that she taught out of our garage studio. So I've been around girls all my life and never really got the macho guy thing."

As they spent more time together, their feelings grew more intense. "Neither of us had ever been in a relationship before, so we took things slow," says Emily. "But after the six-month mark, we both kind of realized that it was serious, even though we hadn't actually said the I-love-you thing yet."

One topic they discussed openly was whether or not they wanted to lose their virginity. "After we became more serious, it was an issue," says Emily. "We talked about it and decided we wanted to wait to have sex." Adds Josh, "It's just not something we want to do right now." They reached this decision together, and their commitment has brought them closer. "While most couples think it's crazy, it only makes our relationship stronger," she notes.

"It's not like we walk around with a sign—'We haven't had sex,'" says Josh. "But when people are talking and it does come up, they're, like, 'How long have you guys been going out?' They're pretty amazed."

But the pair doesn't worry about what other people think. "It's like everyone thinks it's rare not to be having sex on a regular basis," she says. "But with us, we both feel lucky to have each other."

Pure Entertainment

The couple is constantly looking for ways to have fun together. "We both like to be dorky and funny," admits Emily. "We have the same sense of humor. And we laugh and joke around a lot." Often, they amuse themselves by sharing a pie at their favorite table at Frankie's Pizza and Pasta, or simply going to pick flowers on a nearby farm. Both dog-lovers, they enjoy taking Emily's puppy—a golden Lab named

Ruby—for strolls around the neighborhood dog park.

Since it was a photo that first brought the couple together, it's only fitting that they love to take pictures. A year ago, they discovered a black-and-

Together for two years, Josh and Emily share something special and make each other happy.

white photo booth that they visit every few months. For Valentine's Day, Emily surprised Josh with shots from "their booth" of her holding up signs with messages for him. Josh has also pulled off some creative stunts. Following Emily's graduation, he snuck into her house while she was sleeping. Using a Polaroid camera, he took pictures of himself and hid them around her room so that she could wake up to his smiling face.

In the summer of 2000, Emily and Josh went to California on a three-week vacation with his family. The highlight of the trip was attending a friend of the family's wedding on a pirate ship in Long Beach. To play along with a medieval theme, Emily and Josh went clad in authentic 1700s garb designed for the occasion. "It was so much fun picking out the styles and dressing up like a couple right out of medieval times," she says excitedly. "The whole trip was a blast. Even something as dirty as riding dune buggies was romantic because we found little ways to make it so."

Emily and Josh believe that their relationship has been a positive influence on their lives. "I can share things with Emily that I don't share with anybody else," says Josh. "Before I met her, I was going down this path. And now that I look back, I can see it wasn't good. I would be totally different right now if I hadn't met Emily." Emily agrees: "I think we've helped each other in a lot of ways—we've kept each other sane. And we make each other happy."

Kristi Piel, 17
VIRGINIA BEACH, VIRGINIA

Jay Maxwell, 17
ARLINGTON, VIRGINIA

Kristi, who loves to sing and perform, understands what it's like to have stage fright. On a church retreat in December 1998, she was backstage before the talent show began when she spotted a guy having a classic case of stage fright. He was wearing only a towel to play the role of "The Peach" for a comedy skit. He was so nervous, he asked her to give him a hand. Kristi agreed and, right on cue, she shoved him out onto the stage. His act was a complete success, and she hoped they'd meet again.

Getting Acquainted Offstage

At breakfast the following day, a friend introduced Kristi to Jay, whom she immediately recognized as "The Peach." The two started chatting and quickly bonded over similar interests and shared values.

"I thought she was the coolest person in the world," recalls Jay. "We talked about everything from family to favorite songs and movies. We had a lot in common, so we really hit it off. The chemistry was perfect." He confessed that, two years earlier, he had heard her sing at a talent show and was so blown away, he had looked for her after the performance but couldn't track her down. Now it seemed as if they were destined to meet.

Kristi felt completely comfortable around him. "He was a great listener and treated me with so much respect, I felt like a princess," she says. "I felt like I could have told him my life story and not have to worry about a thing." They were inseparable for the rest of the trip.

After the retreat, the two kept in touch with a stream of letters and phone calls. As they got to know each other better, they became the closest of friends who leaned on each other during difficult times. Whenever Kristi was upset, she would call Jay for advice and support, and vice versa.

Passage to Love

It wasn't until a year later that their friendship developed into something more. Just before the next retreat, Kristi and Jay were talking on the phone. "I said that I didn't want to go to the pool because I looked fat," recalls Kristi. Jay insisted that she stop saying that and said, "I don't care what you look like, because . . . " She pressed: "Because what?" And he responded, "Because Kristi, I love you."

Hearing those words, Kristi started crying. "That was the first time I'd ever been told 'I love you' from a guy and I really believed him," she says. "There was no doubt in my mind that I felt the same way. I was just like, whoa, this near-perfect guy likes me."

Why did it take the couple so long to reveal their true feelings? "I wanted to pursue a relationship, but I was hesitant because it was long distance," explains Jay. "But over time, that just kept fading. The more I thought about it, the more I realized that I loved her. At first I was too scared to say anything. Finally, I said, 'Screw it, I'm going for it.'"

Taking It Slow

At the retreat, Kristi and Jay were so excited to see each other, they were glued to each other's sides. During one break, they ended up in an elevator by themselves. Jay gave Kristi a hug and stood there just looking at her. "I was, like, 'What are you waiting for?'" recalls Kristi. "He said, 'Is it okay to kiss you?' And I said, 'You don't have to wait for that.'" Then he smiled and kissed her.

"It was like fireworks," says Jay. "I knew then I wanted to keep her in my life for a good long while." Kristi agrees that it was a turning point. "I was speechless," she says. "I've had a troubled history with guys and I told Jay about that. So he wasn't pushy. He cared about what I wanted. It was really awesome because I found out what kind of guy he was in that moment. And I was hooked into love."

Support System

That love has carried them through good—and tough—times. "I've had a lot of self-esteem problems," says Kristi. "Jay's helped put a whole new outlook on life. Now I know there is someone who loves me. I still have my down times, but he's always there to bring me up. He's very understanding, and a great listener."

"I try to change her attitude from being sad to being happy," says Jay. "If she needs me, she knows I will stop everything to be with her. And I know when the chips are down, there's this one person who is always there for me. No matter what, we'll be there for each other. We just have this unconditional love."

Yen Nguyen, 17

Gilbert Ayala, 17

VIRGINIA BEACH, VIRGINIA

The first time freshman Gilbert Ayala spotted Yen Nguyen in PE class, he was so captivated by her million-watt smile, he knew he had to meet her. So he did what any guy in a love-induced trance would do: He sat in her seat.

"What are you doing?" Yen rebuffed him. "Get out of my spot."

Though this first encounter didn't go as smoothly

as he had hoped, Gilbert mustered the nerve to approach her again. The second time, they hit it off and became good friends. Even though Gilbert was interested in Yen, he didn't dare reveal the true nature of his feelings yet.

"It was a secret crush," admits Gilbert. Adds Yen, "I had a crush on him, too. But he didn't give me any clues, so neither one of us said anything."

The Mating Dance

During sophomore year, they communicated their mutual interest by telling their friends. Yen was thrilled by the news and wanted to start dating immediately. "I kept hinting that we should be boyfriend and girlfriend," says Yen. "But he never responded."

Gilbert had some reservations about diving into a relationship; though reluctant to admit it, he was still deeply hurt by his last relationship. "I wasn't ready to start trusting people," he says. "So I was being cautious. I wanted to be with Yen, but I didn't want to make her my girlfriend yet." So he dodged her questions and avoided any discussions about getting serious.

Baffled by his reaction, Yen took his actions as a rejection and stopped speaking to him. "At the time, I didn't know that he was really hurt by an old

Once Gilbert and Yen established themselves as a couple, they became inseparable.

girlfriend. So I got really mad," she says. After a few weeks passed and things had calmed down, they resumed talking and became close again. But before things could escalate, Gilbert would pull away. This

Voted senior class couple, they are admired by others for always having fun together.

cycle repeated throughout the year.

By December of their junior year, Yen was tired of waiting for Gilbert to ask her out. So she took matters into her own hands: She marched right up to him and asked him to go with her to an upcoming dance.

Gilbert wanted to say "yes," but he held his tongue. He had his reasons, but kept Yen in the dark. "I was embarrassed about not having money, but I didn't want to tell her why," says Gilbert. "So I said I didn't know if I could go."

Though Yen was crushed by his response, she hoped he'd change his mind. Unbeknownst to her, Gilbert sought out work so that he could accept her invitation. "I got a job just so that I could save money for the dance," Gilbert explains.

A month before the dance, Gilbert succeeded in his mission and was finally ready to follow his heart. "After we had been talking for a long time, I realized that I trusted her," he says. "I thought if I didn't ask her out now, I was going to lose her for good." So he called Yen up and simply said, "Can I ask you a question? Will you be my girlfriend?" Without missing a beat, she happily agreed.

Love Lessons

Attending the dance together, they capped off their courtship with a thrilling evening that surpassed their expectations—and marked a happy beginning. Ever since, the pair has been inseparable and no longer hides their feelings from each other. Voted senior class couple, this duo learned that love is worth the wait.

Yen and Gilbert argue that the best relationships

"I think we fell in love as friends," Gilbert and Yen say.

begin with a solid friendship. "If you're friends before you start dating, you can find out a lot about a person," Yen notes. "Most couples start dating and then, later on, find out stuff they don't like. But if you're friends, you *know* each other." Gilbert agrees: "You get to know the real them. I think we fell in love as friends."

Finding out whom you can really count on, says Yen, is also an important part of any relationship. "When I broke my arm twice while cheerleading within three months, Gilbert was there for me the whole time—at the doctor's, during surgery. I got really depressed, but he was always there to support me and make me feel better. He took care of me and brought me food and played Monopoly."

Gilbert says that Yen has also taught him about the meaning of love: "I don't really trust that many people. When I started going out with Yen, I learned to trust better, and that trust has just kept growing."

Chapter 2

opposites
ATTRACT

On the surface, these couples seem like
unlikely pairs, but they prove that
love can bridge all differences.

Renée Krajcik, 19

Justin Ridenour, 17

BELLINGHAM, MASSACHUSETTS

Though he was a freshman and she was a junior, Justin was not intimidated by the age difference and asked Renée to go out with him. At first, her friends teased her about his underclassman status. "They were, like, 'You're going out with a freshman?'" she recalls. "But once I got to know Justin, I really liked him. He had a great sense of humor and personality. So I didn't care what they thought."

What first drew them together was their love of music. They met in band practice: She played the clarinet; he played the baritone saxophone. Justin noticed Renée right away. "She just stuck out compared to all the other girls," he says. "I liked that she was intelligent and could make me laugh. She intrigued me."

Their mutual love of music brought Renée and Justin together.

Renée and Justin went out for a month, but the romance quickly fizzled. She felt that he wasn't interested in spending time with her and avoided making plans. After only a handful of dates, Renée called it quits. "I never had a boyfriend before," she explains. "When I suspected he was going to end things, I made sure I beat him to it."

Attitude Adjustment

At a school dance three months later, the two were barely on speaking terms. But important things had been left unsaid and feelings were unresolved. "When I saw Justin at the dance, I realized how much I missed him," says Renée. "All night I wanted Justin to sweep me off my feet for one heavenly dance, but it never happened. That night I realized I needed him in my life more than anything."

Justin had a similar revelation. The next day, he called Renée and asked her for a second chance. He confessed that on the night of the dance, he'd thought she was the most beautiful angel he had ever seen, and realized for the first time that he loved her.

A Case of Complements

This time, the couple promised to improve their relationship and work out any problems together. By trusting each other, their differences have made them stronger. Once shy and reserved, Renée says that Justin's outgoing personality has helped boost her confidence level. "Before I met Justin, I had very low self-esteem and was extremely introverted," she says.

By trusting each other, their differences have made them stronger.

"I'm really shy around people I don't know, and Justin's really open. He'll talk to anybody. Since I've been going out with him, he's kind of brought that out in me. He gave me the self-confidence I needed to overcome my shyness."

Likewise, Justin has benefited from Renée's love and support. Justin's schoolwork had been a low priority and he scooted by with C's and D's. But Renée's influence helped him reform his bad habits and he began acing tests and getting A's and B's. "She helps me whenever I need it," he says. "I didn't used to study much, but after I met Renée, I became a lot more studious. Our personalities just click together—that's why everything fits right."

Surprise Endings

Even when the pair doesn't see eye to eye, they're able to find common ground. One time, Renée was extremely mad at Justin for flirting with someone else and wouldn't speak to him all day. That night, at a school dance, Justin borrowed the deejay's mike and apologized to her in front of the whole school. He said, "I really messed up with my girlfriend today and I just want to say, Renée, I'm so sorry and I hope you will forgive me. I love you."

Whether it's camping, skiing, dancing or just hanging out, Renée and Justin always make time for each other and the activities they love.

Renée was speechless. "My heart just melted," she recalls. "I definitely forgave him then and there. He's never been afraid to tell or show people how he feels about me."

It's important, says Justin, for Renée to know how much he cares about her. For their eight-month anniversary, he surprised her with a present. "When I opened up this little box, there was a gold locket," she remembers. "Justin had written me a note that it was his heart and as long as I kept it with me, he would always be there for me. And I haven't taken it off yet."

Trusting Instincts

Three years later, that promise—to be there for each other—still holds true. Even though Renée attends college fifty miles away, they always make time for each other and the activities they love, like swing dancing and listening to music.

The couple believes that their relationship is built on a foundation of trust and communication. "We're very open about our emotions and how we're feeling. If there's something bothering us, we can always let the other person know and they'll help make it better," explains Renée. "It's really important to be able to trust the other person. If I didn't trust

Justin, there's no way this relationship would work out." Justin agrees: "That's totally key. You need to trust the person and talk. If you can't talk, then it's just pointless. Like I love talking to Renée. That's what I look forward to every day."

Robin Godfrey, 20

Jamie Bourden, 20

GRINNELL, IOWA

Robin and Jamie are a perfect example of a love connection that began with few factors in common. An art major, Robin is intensely passionate about painting and drawing. On the other end of the spectrum is Jamie, a physics major, who is a whiz at anything related to math or science.

During the fall of their freshman year at Grinnell College, Robin and Jamie lived in the same dorm. Introduced by mutual friends, they started hanging out regularly. Despite their different interests, they formed a bond and became close friends. "We spent a lot of nights staying up talking, just the two of us," he remembers.

"I had a crush on her," Jamie admits, "but I knew she had a boyfriend back home. So I tried to set my feelings aside and be content with being friends." Though it was trying at times, he played it cool. By the spring, Robin had broken up with her boyfriend, but she still wasn't aware of Jamie's interest.

At a school formal, Jamie wanted to make his intentions clear. He was dancing with a friend when he spotted Robin; he suggested they switch partners. "I figured I'd give it a shot," he says, "and things worked out pretty well." Once the pair started dancing, they couldn't tear themselves apart.

That night, the two shared their first kiss. Since then, the couple has found out the real meaning of love. "We became pretty serious pretty fast," Robin recalls. In the first month they were together, they had a big hurdle to overcome: Robin had already made plans to work in her hometown of Acme, Washington, for the summer and the fall semester. That meant they would be hundreds of miles apart for a nine-month stretch. Committed to the relationship, they vowed to stay together.

Factoring in the Distance

"When you're in a long-distance relationship, it's hard not to let stressful things outside our relationship affect us," says Jamie. "And it can bring a lot of things to the surface or amplify things that we wouldn't worry about otherwise." Ditto, says Robin: "It's just so frustrating not being able to see the other person and talk in person. So that frustration just builds."

How did they work out these issues? "We kept in contact as much as possible," says Jamie. "We traded daily e-mails back and forth and talked every two or three days. We knew what we had to do to keep things going." They relied on each other for support and comfort. "Just hearing his voice helped me a lot," says Robin.

The couple maintains that though it was challenging to be apart, they learned a lot from the experience. "Going through the long distance has only strengthened our relationship," notes Robin. "If we can make it through that, we can make it through anything."

Over fall break, Jamie visited Robin in Washington, an experience he'll never forget. "The thing that made me feel the closest to Robin was meeting her family and finding out where she grew up," he says. "She has a house in the woods and I've always dreamed of having a small house in the woods. Seeing where she lived and finding it so beautiful made me feel extremely close to her."

Though long-distance love is challenging, it makes being together even sweeter!

Finding Common Ground

Though Robin and Jamie approach problems differently, they help each other see eye to eye. "Right off the bat, we look at things in different ways," he says. "I like to pick them apart and find reasons and patterns." Robin, on the other hand, trusts her gut. "I make decisions more on feelings and intuition, less on reason," she says. "But I think that makes our relationship more interesting. Like pieces of a puzzle, we are shaped differently, but fit together perfectly."

They've discovered that these differences enhance their relationship and open them up to new experiences. With Robin's encouragement, Jamie has tapped into his artistic side and delved into writing poetry. "Being with Robin has brought a lot of inspiration," he says.

True Romance

In the past year, what the pair has learned goes a lot deeper than opposites attracting. "The best part of our relationship," says Robin, "is the degree of honesty and openness we've achieved." Jamie believes that the truth is absolutely critical for happiness. "I've had relationships in the past where honesty wasn't there all the time," he says. "So I know how much that can hurt. If you're not honest, you don't really know the person you're with." Emphasizes Robin, "It's not just honesty as in not telling a lie, but [as in] sharing everything and not holding anything back."

"I never really knew what it was like to be in love," says Jamie. "I may have thought I did, but this is so different. I didn't know what a fulfilling relationship was like until now." Agrees Robin, "This is definitely something very unique. It just feels right." Says Jamie, "Yes, like everything just falls into place and we're both completely happy. You don't have to question it."

through thick
& THIN

Two couples share how their love survived
despite some of life's toughest challenges.

Catherine Nguyen, 22

Sinh Luong, 23

LONG BEACH, CALIFORNIA

When Catherine and Sinh first met at the public library in the fall of 1994, they felt an immediate connection. "My friends were trying to pick her up," recalls Sinh, "and she just started talking to me. It was like we knew each other before." Catherine agrees: "It was strange, but I felt like I knew him, in a past life or something. I don't know why, but I trusted him immediately."

The pair's first outing started on shaky ground.

"It was my first time driving my car on my own, and I went in all the wrong directions," explains Sinh with a laugh. "At the mall parking lot, I kept stopping and backing up. I was so nervous, I started shaking." But Catherine was a good sport about the whole experience: "I teased him and was, like, 'Oh, my God, don't you know how to drive?'"

More than Friends

For the next two years, Catherine and Sinh were the best of friends. As upperclassmen from different high schools, the pair talked on the phone every night, shared everything with each other and hung out together with friends on the weekends. They also traded long letters, writing about whatever was on their minds.

But while Sinh knew he had feelings for Catherine, she thought of him as a brother. "I never saw him as more than a friend," she admits. "I never thought I'd go for him because he was my best friend." Sinh, however, was optimistic about a future together. "Our friendship helped us through all the bad times and we always talked about being friends for life," he says. "I kept hoping that one day she might see things differently."

Lucky Charm

For her seventeenth birthday, Catherine threw a party and the celebration got out of hand. Uninvited guests showed up at her house, presents were stolen—the cops even had to break up the festivities. On what should have been a happy occasion, Catherine was hurt and devastated.

But the next night, Sinh gave her a gift that changed her mood—and her life. He took off his jade necklace, placed it around her neck and said, "As long as you wear this, you'll always be protected, and I'll always be here for you." Catherine fell for him then and there.

"I was in tears," she recalls. "At that moment, I saw him differently and it made me realize that no guy has ever been this sweet to me. He's really been there for me." As they started dating, everything fell into place effortlessly. Says Catherine, "He makes me feel like a princess."

Positive Payoff

On the surface, the couple's personalities are as different as night and day. "I'm the quiet type," admits Sinh. "I like to draw, write poetry or rent a movie for the evening." Catherine prefers more social activities. "I'm the hyper one," she asserts. "I'm the kind of

Once Catherine and Sinh started dating, everything just fell into place.

person who likes hanging out with friends, going out and dancing. We're totally opposite." But, notes Sinh, "We balance each other out."

And they're always in tune with each other.

Catherine says Sinh has a sixth sense when it comes to her emotions. "Sometimes when I'm down, he knows it. He can feel it," she insists. Sinh agrees: "It works both ways. I'm hard to read a lot of the time, but she can always call my mood. When I'm down, she helps me a lot."

Five years later, they're students at Cal State University at Long Beach, but some things haven't changed. They're still best friends who turn to each other for everything. "To have a good relationship, you have to understand each other as friends," says Sinh. "Be sure to build a good foundation." Adds Catherine, "Talk about the future. Sinh's always meant a lot to me, but now I can't see my life without him. I know he's the one for me."

Ann-Margaret Brannon, 19

John Swearingen, 22

COLUMBIA, SOUTH CAROLINA

They've been together just over two years, but in that short time Ann-Margaret Brannon and John Swearingen have had their love and commitment to each other tested in ways that most couples don't experience in a lifetime. In May 1996, John was first diagnosed with a rare cancerous tumor called PNET that attacks bone and soft tissue. He had countless rounds of chemotherapy, surgery to remove one tumor and, last fall, a life-threatening stem-cell transplant.

All the while, Ann-Margaret has been at his side, cheering him on and supporting him through each painful episode. It has been an emotional—and, at times, desperate—ordeal, but one that has made their bond that much stronger. In the end, says Ann-Margaret, "What gets you through is unconditional love."

Meeting with Destiny

Their love story began in January 1999, when Ann-Margaret, then a senior at Spartanburg High in Spartanburg, South Carolina, was surfing the Internet and came across John's Web site. She noticed that John was a sophomore at the same college her brother attended, and e-mailed him a compliment on his page design. By April, they were chatting nightly; three weeks later, they agreed to meet in person.

For their first official date, John picked Ann-Margaret up at her house (where he also met with her mom's approval), then took her to dinner. There, John told Ann-Margaret how he'd survived cancer in high school. "It was a big part of my life," he says. "If I was going to date this girl, this was an issue I had to get out there." For her part, Ann-Margaret "was so touched" that he'd told her about his cancer. "After he dropped me off," she says, "I was floating. I knew that we were meant for each other."

Tough Times Ahead

By the end of June, they were inseparable, and Ann-Margaret went with John for his six-month routine checkup—a necessary precaution, even though he'd been cancer-free for two years. This time the tests revealed a new soft-tissue tumor in John's chest.

"Hearing the numbers was terrifying," admits Ann-Margaret. "The first time, the doctors told him he had a seventy percent chance of survival. Now he only had thirty percent." Says John, "You're never prepared for news like that. Everything in my life stopped right then."

Battling It Together

They discussed what the diagnosis meant for their relationship. "John told me, 'I understand if you don't need this in your life,'" remembers Ann-Margaret. "But I didn't want to give up on us. I told him, 'If you're willing to stick with us, then so am I.'" John was willing, too: "I really wanted her to be there. There was a lot going on, and it made it easier having somebody to really talk to."

The second time John was diagnosed with cancer, Ann-Margaret told him, "If you're willing to stick with us, then so am I."

A week later, John had surgery to remove the tumor; four months of chemotherapy followed. Then in November, he underwent a stem-cell transplant, a grueling, monthlong procedure that left him near death. The recovery was almost as bad, says John, who spent three weeks in an isolated area of the hospital in his hometown, Columbia, where few visitors were allowed. "If you got any kind of infection, you would probably die," he says. "I couldn't even leave the room. It was pretty trying."

During those weeks, Ann-Margaret, who had just started her freshman year at the University of South Carolina (also in Columbia), shuttled back and forth between classes and the hospital. "I've always been a caregiver," says Ann-Margaret, who would bring John Chinese food and hold his hand at night. "I decided whatever John needs from me, I'll be there for him." She adds, "It definitely changed my life."

It also changed the way they felt about each other, bringing them closer and, in turn, helping them cope with the rigors of John's disease. "When you love someone, all the things that seem imperfect to people on the outside just go away," John says. "You know the other person's going to love you no matter what."

Still, admits Ann-Margaret, "Things got really grim. I didn't think I'd ever see him walking around, or with hair again. But you find the strength somewhere and just persevere," she adds, "praying that one day everything's going to be okay."

Surviving Another Round

By January, two months after John's transplant, things seemed to be going well. John was recuperating and had enrolled in a class at Ann-Margaret's college. They were even going out to dinner and the movies together—things they hadn't done for months.

Then suddenly, in March, the cancer was back. "Getting the bad news was like falling off a cliff," says John. "The tests showed another spot, the same size as the one that had been removed." This was his third bout, and doctors were worried that John's weakened body couldn't take much more. They sent him to Memorial Sloan-Kettering Cancer Center in New York City, where, with Ann-Margaret's support, he endured yet another heavy dose of radiation and more chemotherapy.

"It was so hard watching him go through that," she says. "I was so scared for him." Being with John helped allay her fears. "When I saw him, I thought, He's real. He's not going anywhere."

But John admits he wasn't so sure. "I was seriously thinking about not doing any more treatment and leaving things up to fate or God," he says. "But I realized there are so many people around me who wouldn't be able to handle seeing me give up." So John hung on. "When you're sick, you realize what really matters," he says. "You can't live your life saying, 'I'm going to do this or that tomorrow,' because there may not be a tomorrow."

Promises to Keep

Finally, in October, things began looking up again: John had finished his chemotherapy and started to regain his strength—thanks in large part to Ann-Margaret. "When things get hard, she keeps me positive," he says. "I know that I can talk to her. And it helps to have someone you can always count on."

While he's "not out of the water," John has resumed classes at Wofford College in Spartanburg, and Ann-Margaret wrapped up her sophomore year in Columbia. Even though they're a hundred miles apart, they still spend every weekend together, and for her nineteenth birthday, John gave Ann-Margaret a promise ring. "It means he's still here and we're moving forward," she says. John couldn't agree more: "I really feel we can spend the rest of our lives together. Everything we've been through together has helped us love each other more."

Chapter 4

against
THE ODDS

No one thought these couples could keep their love going, but their stories show that love can last through the worst of times.

Feather Rogers-Dayton, 21
SEATTLE, WASHINGTON

Ingmar Erler, 21
BERLIN, GERMANY

Over the past two years, Feather has learned that true love has no boundaries or limits. This Seattle native found her soulmate far from home—she met Ingmar in Berlin, Germany. The distance separating the two couldn't break their bond; they promised to love each other through good times and hard times. Feather proved the depth of her love for Ingmar: When he was in a near-fatal accident, she rushed to his side and helped him through a grueling recovery process.

Love's Journey

During her senior year of high school, Feather was a huge fan of Rammstein, a German band. When she found out they were touring Germany in the summer, she wanted to see them play. After getting her parents to agree, she started saving money and planning for the trip. She asked her grade school librarian, who had a lot of contacts in Germany, for advice on places to stay. She put Feather in touch with six families, who agreed to host her during her trip.

In the summer of 1998, Feather had the time of her life traveling around Germany. But seeing Rammstein was not the highlight. During the last leg of her trip, she went to Berlin. At the train station, she was greeted by her host family's son, Ingmar, and became instantly smitten. "He was just the person that was meant for me, and I knew it from the minute I saw him," she recalls. "He was the most incredible guy I'd ever met. I forgot all about Rammstein."

For the next two weeks, Ingmar showed Feather around the city and took her to the places he liked to go. "We had tons and tons of stuff in common," she says. "We shared musical tastes, favorite movies, and a similar sense of humor. We talked for hours and it was like nothing I had ever experienced before." The feeling was mutual. "She was different from other girls I knew," says Ingmar. "It was cool to get to know

From the minute she saw Ingmar, Feather knew he was the one for her.

each other and become really good friends."

But friendship wasn't all that developed. The romantic tension was mounting and a few days before Feather had to leave, she kissed him. "I had to let him know how I felt," she says. "I decided, it's now or never. And we've been locked to each other ever since." Saying good-bye was extremely difficult. "Our feelings for each other were so strong," says Feather. "I couldn't stop crying because I didn't want to leave. I wanted to spend more time with him and he felt the same way."

Though they were thousands of miles apart, they knew they had found something special. "It was really like an angel came and tapped us both on the head and said, 'You will love this person,'" she says. They wrote long letters to each other and racked up large phone bills. In December, Feather went to visit him and they celebrated Christmas and New Year's together. "I've felt love for people before, but never like Ingmar," she explains. "To give it and get it returned to me at the same intensity was amazing."

In February 1999, Ingmar gave Feather the best Valentine's Day present. He came to visit her in Seattle for two weeks. "He passed all the family tests," says Feather. "My parents loved him. My sister Carly, who is the date barometer, loved him, too. She never liked any of my other boyfriends, but she was, like, 'Feather, you got to keep this guy.'"

In June, Feather returned to Berlin to visit Ingmar. After four long months apart, they were ecstatic to see each other. "It was just like heaven to be with him," she says. Though the long-distance relationship could be trying at times, they savored the days they spent together.

Tragedy Strikes

One Saturday morning in November, Feather was expecting a phone call from Ingmar, but instead got some distressing news. "It was all kind of a blur," she recalls. "I heard concerned voices in the other room. When I picked up the phone, Ingmar's mom told me that he was in a bad accident." Ingmar had been hit by a drunk driver while he was walking to the park. Feather was in shock, but she knew she had to do something. "The minute I heard, I decided I had to go there as soon as I could. Just to imagine that I could have lost Ingmar forever nearly destroyed me."

The following day Feather took a flight to Berlin. She was anxious to see Ingmar, but she wasn't prepared for his condition at the hospital. "It was surreal," she says. "You see it all the time on TV, but I had never seen anyone in the hospital like him. He looked awful, like he had been beat up. There were so many machines attached to him he didn't even look human." He had bruises and cuts on his face, bandages around his head and a breathing tube down his throat. "It was so hard to see him like that," says Feather. "I couldn't believe it

Their love for each other was so strong that Feather promised to stay by his side.

was him. I thought, that's not Ingmar—it can't be him. My Ingmar is up and around and well."

But Ingmar was far from well; he was struggling to stay alive. He was in a coma because the accident had caused a major trauma to his head. To save his life, his doctors had to perform risky surgery to reduce the swelling in his brain. "Nobody knew if he was going to survive," says Feather. "We learned later that only fifty percent of the people who have this operation live afterwards."

Slow Recovery

Feather was determined to help Ingmar get better. Every day she visited him at the hospital and kept him company—reading books to him, playing music or simply holding his hand. "I would talk to him and tell him that I love him," she says. "I would tell him that I'm here and I'm going to stay with you. I think it helped him a lot."

It was difficult not knowing when Ingmar would regain consciousness. "There were nights when I would lie awake thinking, 'What is he going to be like when he finally wakes up?'" Feather remembers. "There were plenty of times when I begged a higher life form to put me in that hospital bed instead of Ingmar. I would have gladly traded places with him, had it been possible for me to do so."

Three weeks after the accident, Ingmar started to wake up. He could recognize Feather and his parents, but couldn't communicate with them. Sometimes he would reach out and hold her hand. Or squeeze her hand in response to yes or no questions. "Even though he couldn't tell me, I knew he was happy that I was there," she says. "It was obvious by the huge grin he would get on his face when I would walk into the room. I'd do anything for that smile."

Ingmar's progress was slow, but after a few months, his condition improved significantly, so he moved from the intensive care unit to the rehab clinic. There, they changed the trachea tube in his throat, which freed his vocal cords so that he could speak again. He had to relearn sounds, words and the alphabet. "His first feeble 'hi' was like music to my ears," says Feather. "It was a small miracle after not hearing him for so long."

Feather never thought that taking care of Ingmar was a sacrifice. "I knew that he needed me badly," she says. "I was going to stay there with him because nothing else was as important as his well-being. I always stressed that I wouldn't leave him. I just let him know that I would be there for him and nothing would change that."

But it was a long and challenging path ahead. "One of the hardest things for me to see was his helplessness," says Feather. "He was like a baby who had to learn everything again. I was there helping him to learn how to walk and eat again. I took him outside in his wheelchair for fresh air and sun, and eventually we took slow walks together. Every day brought with it a small triumph." Ingmar appreciated all of her efforts. "He was really glad that I was there," she says. "I knew he was getting back to his old self when he started to laugh again. His personality was still there."

In May, six months after his accident, Ingmar finally returned home. He went to therapy three times a week and worked on skills that he had trouble with, like speaking, reading and writing. With time and perseverance, not to mention Feather's help, he found his way back to his old life—and a happier place.

Love Lessons

"It changed my life," says Feather. "I knew I was capable of a tremendous love, but really you don't have any idea until it happens. When you love someone, you don't give up if it gets a little hard. You carry on through everything that life throws at you—be it good or bad. It's not easy, but it's worth it."

Despite the hardships they've faced, Feather and Ingmar's love has persevered. "It's not easy, but it's worth it," says Feather.

Now Feather is back in Seattle and Ingmar is in Germany. Even though they are so far apart, they are looking forward to a future together. She is interested in sewing and clothing design; he wants to pursue drawing and art school. Together, they know they are capable of anything. "I've always known in my heart that Ingmar is The One for me," says Feather. "You don't often hear the fairy-tale version of love. I have found a modern-day fairy tale in my love for Ingmar and his love for me."

Jamie Dwyer, 20

Jamah Perry, 22

EVANSVILLE, INDIANA

When Jamie Dwyer started her freshman year at the University of Evansville, love was the farthest thing from her mind. She had no inkling that she was about to meet the guy of her dreams. She also never anticipated that her relationship would cause a painful rift with her family. She was about to learn the power of love—and it would change her life forever.

Budding Romance

As a new student on campus, Jamie mingled with so many different people, it was hard to keep everyone's name and face straight. But one person made a lasting impression: a junior named Jamah. "When I first saw him, I knew I wanted to talk to him," says Jamie, who noticed him at a party. That night they spoke for only a few minutes, but many conversations would follow.

Over the next three months, they had long heart-to-hearts, sharing stories and important details from their lives. "She was very easy to talk to," says Jamah. "We talked about all kinds of stuff, but mostly about relationships." Jamie even confided in him about potential dates. "I was seeking advice about other guys, but all I wanted to do was talk to him," she explains.

"I was very nervous," admits Jamah. "I was never the ladies' man type, so I didn't think she'd ever be attracted to me. That's why it took me so long to go to the next level from friends." Right before winter break, Jamah finally worked up the nerve to make it clear he was interested in more than friendship. "Our first kiss was so cute and innocent," recalls Jamie. "He kept stalling and wouldn't let me leave his room. Finally, he said good-bye at the door, hugged me and gave me this little pop kiss!" "It was just a little peck," he says. "Since we were both leaving town, we needed to do something so we'd know where we stood in the future."

Secrets and Revelations

"During break, all I could think about was Jamah," Jamie says. "That's when I knew it was getting serious. From my past relationships, I knew what I wanted. With Jamah, we connected on a totally different level. I knew he was *it*." Returning from break, she and Jamah spent a lot of time together. The more she got to know him, the stronger she felt. "I was falling in love with him," she says.

Still, Jamie did have doubts about the future of the relationship. She knew that her parents wouldn't approve of dating Jamah because he's African-American. Ever since she was young, they had preached to steer clear of interracial relationships. "My dad always said to me, 'You can be friends, but just never date. You better not even *think* about dating a black guy,'" she says. That's how he was raised, she explains, and he thought interracial dating spelled trouble.

So in the beginning Jamie kept their romance hidden from her family. It wasn't easy, because she saw them three or four times a week. They live near campus, so she stopped by the house to have dinner,

At first, Jamie kept her relationship with Jamah a secret, but after a while it became too hard to ignore her feelings for him.

do laundry, or just to chat. "It was so incredibly hard to keep Jamah a secret," she says. "He had become a huge part of my life. Not being able to share something that important in your life with your parents is an awful feeling."

Jamie desperately wanted to share her happy news with her family. Since she had always been close with her mom, she decided to tell her about Jamah. "I was worried," she says, "but she's very supportive of anything I choose to do. Once she saw how happy he made me, she was there for me."

Jamie knew her dad would be harder to win over. Three months passed before she made up her mind to tell him. She didn't think there would ever be a right time, but she wanted to be honest with him. In April, she wrote him a letter explaining her relationship and her feelings for Jamah. She hoped he could understand and be happy for her.

Nuclear Reaction

As soon as Jamie's father read her letter, all hell broke loose. He was furious that she had disobeyed him and wasn't about to tolerate her defiance. He issued an ultimatum: As long as she stayed in a relationship with Jamah, he would cut off all ties with her.

Jamie was devastated by her dad's reaction. Even though she knew he'd be upset, she never imagined how far he would go. "It was terrible. He more or less disowned me," she recalls. "He went to the extreme and wouldn't listen to anyone." He stopped speaking to her, refused to pay for her education and banned her from the house. He demanded that her mother and sister do the same and shut her out of their lives completely.

"My family was torn apart," says Jamie. "We were so unbelievably close. To hear everyone arguing and all the hatred hurt tremendously." Her mom and sister sided with Jamie, but her father wouldn't budge. The arguments escalated. "My mom and sister were ready to go to war for me," she says. "It got really bad. At one point they were going to make my dad pack his bags and move out."

It was her worst nightmare, Jamie recalls. "It was turmoil," she says. "I would cry at night just thinking about everything. I was worried my parents would split up and I would never see my dad again. I was also worrying about how I was going to pay for school. I didn't know what I was going to do."

Believing in Love

Jamie faced an unbearable decision: choosing between her family and the guy she loved. "It was so hard, because I knew all I had to do was cut my relationship off with Jamah," she says. "But I couldn't. I loved him and I wasn't going to give up the person who brought so much happiness and joy into my life."

Jamah also felt like he was stuck in a no-win situation: "I wasn't comfortable knowing that I was the cause of domestic upheaval. I thought maybe I should end the relationship and look out for her family." He hoped that Jamie's father would change his mind or at least give him a chance. "I was embarrassed for him and his attitude," he says. "He never even met me, yet he wouldn't have anything to do with me."

Jamie knew she couldn't turn her back on love, but it was stressful to be cut off from her family. The next few months were an emotional roller coaster. Whenever she got upset, she turned to Jamah. "I cried a lot and he was there through everything. He's the best friend," she says. He stayed by her side and comforted her nonstop. "We needed to support each other," explains Jamah. "It was really my job to make sure she was okay and let her know we'd get through it and that love conquers all."

Deep down, Jamie knew she was making the right decision by following her heart. She believed that it was more important to see people for who they really are—not judge them by their skin color. "You have to take the time to get to know a person on the inside," she says, "and accept the fact that we're all the same. We all have emotions and the ability to love. I know that love is color blind."

Change of Heart

Three months later, in July, Jamie's father woke up one morning, thought he was having a heart attack and was taken to the hospital. It turned out to be a false alarm, but the experience shook him up. "He called me and told me he wanted to see me," Jamie says, "because he did not want to die with us on bad terms."

Jamie was relieved and happy to hear his words. While she was still hurt by his actions, she was ready to move on. "I missed him a great deal," she says. "I forgave him right away because I understood where he was coming from. It's hard to go against everything you were brought up to believe." They had many open talks over the next few weeks. She knew that he was serious about starting anew when he asked to be introduced to Jamah. "It was really scary," admits Jamah, "because all of a sudden he wanted to meet me. But I respected him for being able to change his mind-set." This meeting was a step in the right direction, says Jamie, because she knew it was difficult for her dad to swallow his pride. "It took a lot of work, but he was slowly coming around," she says.

With time, her dad has even grown to appreciate Jamah. "Now he's a lot more accepting of our relationship," says Jamie. "He truly is seeing Jamah as I see him and not judging him by his skin color." Adds Jamah, "He sat me down one day and said, 'I think very highly of you and I've never seen Jamie this happy. I can see it's because of you and I just want to say thanks and I'm

Jamie and Jamah both believe their relationship has grown stronger because of all they've gone through.

sorry for what I put you guys through earlier.'"

"It's really an amazing turnaround," says Jamah, who feels their love has deepened through their efforts and understanding. "Jamie's like my other half—just being around her makes me happy." Jamie agrees completely. "Our relationship was put to the test. Jamah's my soul mate and I love him with all my heart. After what we went through, we can make it through anything."

Chapter 5

LOVE
connections

Through common interests, these couples have
formed a bond held together with love.

Terese Opiela, 19

Brian Jones, 18

BUTLER, NEW JERSEY

Terese was never the type to believe in psychics. But in July 1999, she had an experience that made her change her mind. One of her friends threw a party and invited a psychic to do readings for all the guests. Though she was skeptical, Terese decided to play along and have her fortune told. Right off the bat the psychic surprised her by revealing personal details about Terese's family. How could she possibly guess my brother was adopted?

she thought. Then the psychic told her about her love life: Terese would meet a guy for the second time, and they would become really close. He would be tall, have brown hair, be younger than her and his name would begin with B. Oddly, she predicted he would be complaining about his haircut when they met. But most importantly, he would "treat her like a princess." Terese racked her brain for anyone who could fit this description, but she didn't really take the prediction seriously.

The next night, Terese and a group of friends hung out at a local coffeehouse. She noticed that a guy named Brian kept glancing her way. (They had met a few months earlier when she went with a mutual friend to his school's prom.) When he started complaining about his new haircut, Terese did a double take. It was the exact line the psychic had predicted he would use to talk to her. "It was so weird," she says. "I was, like, 'Oh, my God, that's crazy.' I didn't believe in psychics, so I just thought she couldn't be right." But the psychic's words turned out to be eerily close to reality.

For the rest of the summer, Terese and Brian saw each other almost every night. At first, they hung out with other friends, but soon they started talking one-on-one by phone and online. "I felt a connection with her," says Brian. "I just wanted to hang out with her more and get to know her. When we talked, we never ran out of conversation. We just clicked." According to Terese, they felt comfortable opening up to each other: "We talked about everything—school, movies, our families. We became best friends."

Brian wanted to tell Terese how he felt about her, but he wasn't sure how to do it. "I was always bashful," he says. "Honestly, I'd never been good with girls. I was always afraid to ask a girl out." But with Terese, he knew it was time to take a risk. "I was thinking about her all the time," he says. "I was so nervous about telling her I liked her. But I had to get it off my chest." Much to his relief, she put his fears at ease and agreed to be his girlfriend. "It took a lot of guts to tell me," she says. "When he said, 'I really like you,' it made me feel differently about him. I felt like I could trust him with anything."

Making the Connection

When school started up in September, the couple spent less time together because they attended different high schools. But they still talked regularly and enjoyed doing activities together. She would go to his hockey games; he would go to her dance competitions. On

Brian credits their relationship for helping him overcome his shyness.

weekends, they would often meet up for a movie, or play video games and air hockey at the arcade. They also liked to go in-line skating and mini-golfing. Sometimes they would split a hot fudge sundae at the local ice-cream shop. "We have the best times together," says Terese. "We're really active and we like to have fun."

By the time Christmas break rolled around, they had been together for almost four months. One night, they were chatting on-line and Terese asked him, "How much do you like me?" "I told her, 'I like you more than all the stars in the sky,'" recalls Brian. "It was a joking statement, but I kind of meant it. When she didn't take it seriously, I took it the wrong way and told her I had to go." Terese was confused by his behavior, but the following day, Brian cleared things up. "I told her I loved her," he says. " I wanted to take the next step in our relationship."

"I was completely surprised," says Terese. "I didn't know he felt that way about me. He definitely showed me, but I didn't expect him to say it." Though she was falling in love with him, she wasn't ready to repeat the words. "I didn't want to say it just because he'd said it. I wanted to say it when I really felt it," she explains. A week later, Terese told Brian she loved him.

Love Lessons

The couple says they've learned a lot from each other, even though they have very different personalities. "I'm more outgoing than Brian," notes Terese. "Because I'm a dancer, I'm used to going out onstage in front of a bunch of people." Brian says, "I'm more self-conscious. I just need more reassurance to let go and not care what other people think." He credits their relationship for helping him overcome his shyness. "Terese gave me a lot of confidence in myself," he says. "She will back me up whenever I'm feeling insecure. I used to be a push-over and wanted to please everyone. Now, I won't let anybody walk all over me."

Even though they attend different high schools, Brian and Terese still find time to spend together.

Likewise, Terese says their relationship has made her feel more secure. "I've learned from Brian that I can be my complete self all the time. He always makes me feel good. Every time I thought something wouldn't work out, he would prove me wrong." Adds Brian, "I can trust Terese with anything and I know she'll always be there for me. Even when she's having a bad day, I know I can always turn to her."

Maria Alejandra Navas, 19

Enrique ("Rico") Iribarren, 20

MIAMI, FLORIDA

Maria comes from a very tight-knit family. She and her two sisters grew up in Barquisimeto, Venezuela, before moving to Miami when she was eight. She is very close to her parents and is passionate about the Venezuelan culture. So it's always been important to Maria to date someone who understands and embraces her family as well her roots. With Rico, she couldn't have asked for a better match.

In October 1997, Maria and Rico crossed paths at a friend's party. When Maria heard his name, she thought it sounded familiar, like a friend of her family's. She started to ask him questions that included details she remembered about his house and family. "I thought she was stalking me," laughs Rico. But Maria explained that their grandparents are good friends in Venezuela (they live in the same town), and their parents have been friends since childhood. They have even been to each other's houses for special occasions. They have so much in common, it was strange they had never met before.

The following day, Maria, who was excited about making a connection with Rico, got his number from her parents and called him. Although he was surprised to hear from her, he was happy she had decided to get in touch. She invited him to her house, and he agreed to stop by. (It turns out they live on the same street, only five minutes apart.) That night they talked, flirted and shared stories about their families. Under the pretense of studying geometry, Rico visited Maria the next day—and the next. But geometry was far from their minds.

After hanging out for five straight days, the tension was mounting. One night, Maria walked Rico to his car and gave him a hug. Then it seemed like time

Everything fell into place for Maria and Rico.

stopped. "We just looked into each other's eyes and from there we had a pop kiss," recalls Rico. "Then we said good night." Everything was falling into place at a natural pace.

A week later, Rico and Maria watched a movie at his house and as she was leaving, he stopped her and asked sweetly, "Do you want to be my girlfriend?" A delighted Maria could barely contain her excitement. She kissed him and responded, "What do you think?"

Heart to Heart

By December, the two knew they had found something really special. "In one of my classes we had to write in a journal every day," says Rico. "Basically all my entries were about her." Maria was equally crazy about him. "People say you can't fall in love so fast, so I was worried," says Maria. "But I knew how I felt. I told him I loved him." Rico returned the sentiment: "I was head over heels for her from the first moment."

The couple's families were thrilled by the news that the two were dating. Rico visited Maria's house frequently and spent a great deal of time with her family. Her family is more traditional than his is; he was raised more American than Venezuelan. (His mom is Italian; his dad is Venezuelan.) "Maria's parents are very strict," says Rico, "but they trusted me. Because they knew my family, they put a lot of confidence in me."

Rico says that dating Maria has given him a new perspective on Latin culture and helped improve his

Maria has given Rico a new perspective on Latin culture.

Spanish tremendously. "I learned more about having respect and the traditions of Latin families," he says. "For example, when her parents call her by her full name, she has to respond with *Señora* or *Señor*, which is 'ma'am' and 'sir.' That threw me off and took a while to get used to, but now I think it's cool. It shows a sense of respect. I call them *Señor* and *Señora*, too."

In the summer, Maria spent three months with her family in Barquisimeto, Venezuela. This time apart only brought the couple—and their families—closer together. "At first I was upset because I couldn't be with Rico," says Maria. "But I was with his family the whole time. I felt more connected to him. His grandparents even treated me like their grandchild."

After she returned and reunited with Rico, they stayed close to each other's families. One time Rico's father gave him a homemade Venezuelan candy called *melcocha*. "I'd never had it before in my life," he says. "I tasted it and was, like, 'Wow, this is some good stuff.'" He asked his dad to see if their relatives in Venezuela could send more. One of his relatives went in search of the candy but couldn't find it. She asked Rico's grandma for help, but when she didn't have any luck, she asked Maria's grandma. "Maria's grandma ended up calling Maria's house and saying, 'Rico's looking for this candy.' This was all in two days—from here to Venezuela

Both Maria and Rico know they've found something very special.

Though their schedules are full, Maria and Rico
make their relationship a priority.

and back. It just goes to show how tightly our families
are integrated."

Roses and Stargazing

"Rico's very, very romantic," says Maria. "Out
of the blue he'll bring me flowers or chocolates. He

pays attention to little details." For their first Valentine's Day, he brought four roses to the house—one for each of the women in her family, including her mom and two sisters. She was so touched by the way that he included everyone.

Now both Maria and Rico attend Florida International University. She's a public relations major; he is studying information technology. Though their schedules are full, they make their relationship a priority. "School can get hectic sometimes," notes Rico. "If there's time, I'll go surprise her, take her to the park and we'll sit under the stars. We don't have to say a word. As long as she's next to me, I'm so happy. I love to go sit under the stars—it feels like you're in heaven."

Chapter 6

REEL-LIFE
romances

Who says HOLLYWOOD love stories
are too good to be true? Not these couples.
They're playing the lead roles in real-LIFE
versions of some of the hottest romances on
the big and small screens.

by Ellen Lieberman

When Veronica Valencia dragged her childhood friend Nick Casey to see the movie *Boys and Girls* last June, she told him she had found the story of their relationship in the onscreen tale of pals turned lovers. "I was, like, 'We have to see this movie. It's so us,'" recalls Veronica. Adds Nick: "We went, but it was so weird. The whole time they were playing the movie, I knew that she was thinking about us."

That's not surprising, since the film tells the story of two childhood friends, Jennifer and Ryan (played by Claire Forlani and Freddie Prinze, Jr.), who are reluctant to say they're actually in love. Veronica and Nick also met as kids, growing up in Brentwood, California. "We've known each other since elementary school," says Veronica, who became best friends with Nick in high school during their freshman year. "We called and talked to each other every day." They also watched movies, did homework together and even had their own special spot, on a hill overlooking Brentwood. (Remember Jennifer and Ryan's special spot at Vista Point, near the Golden Gate Bridge?) "We were more than just friends but afraid to admit it," Veronica says.

All through high school, they both dated other people. "If she had a boyfriend, and I didn't have a girlfriend, I'd be mad," Nick says. Still, they always managed to support each other. "In the movie [Jennifer] has a problem with her relationship and she talks to [Ryan]," says Veronica. "We were always there for each other, too."

A week after they saw *Boys and Girls*, Nick and Veronica went to their spot, where she told him that maybe she'd been looking too hard for the perfect guy; maybe he was right there in front of her. Nick admits he was a little nervous about the whole idea at first, but he was ultimately happy that she'd confessed her feelings. "We were just talking, and that's when we kissed for the first time," he says.

That kiss led to a romance that convinced Nick to forgo his plans to attend a faraway college, because he "didn't want to leave Veronica." Currently a sophomore at Saint Mary's College of California in Moraga, Nick says that he and Veronica, who's in her second year at nearby Los Medanos College, spend time together just enjoying the "little things." And now that they've been dating for eight months, this boy and girl couldn't be happier with the juicy plot twist in their friendship. As Veronica puts it, "I know it's the right thing."

When it came to choosing a college, Allison Clark weighed the normal factors: the quality of classes, proximity to her Ann Arbor, Michigan, home and—just like *Felicity*'s lead character—the location of her former high school crush. And in the end, just as Felicity (Keri Russell) followed Ben (Scott Speedman) to the University of New York, Allison headed off to Eastern Michigan University in Ypsilanti, Michigan, where her ex-boyfriend, Kyle Ehnis, had gone the year before. She and Kyle had broken up (for the last time) in the winter of 1999, having dated for six months, but he was still on her mind. "I would think to myself that there's always a chance of me running into him on campus," says Allison.

The two met when Allison was a junior and Kyle was a senior at Pioneer High School. Kyle has to admit that he was too shy to make the first move. "I thought she was kind of cute," he says, "but I didn't really talk to her at first." Like the television twosome (who works together at Dean & Deluca), however, Kyle and Allison also had jobs together, at Sears. Before long (and true to the script), Allison's overall "really nice" personality had won him over, and she and Kyle were dating. But when the sparks ultimately stopped flying about a year later in the summer of 1998, the situation became as awkward for them as it was for Ben and Felicity. "On the days that we would both work," Allison recalls, "I'd look out of the corner of my eye or look down as I was walking by [him]." Adds Kyle: "It was a really hard thing, because I knew she wasn't looking at me on purpose."

They began dating other people; Allison even had a boyfriend for a while. But, she says, "I started comparing him to Kyle. It made me realize what a good person [Kyle] was—what I was really missing."

Convinced that she and Kyle should try again, Allison arrived at Eastern Michigan and eventually confessed her feelings to him—that he'd played a role in where she'd decided to go to school. Kyle was flattered but every bit as clueless about Allison's feelings as Ben had been about Felicity's. "It makes me feel good that she was still thinking about me," he says. In June 2000 they reunited, and after all of the ups and downs, Kyle thinks their relationship is as strong as Ben and Felicity's rekindled love. "I feel good about it," he says. "We both want the same things." Allison agrees: "I can look into his eyes and picture our life together."

American Pie

Suhmer Zeiter, 19

Neill Mudano, 20

LAS VEGAS, NEVADA

The *American Pie* scenario where Oz joins the choir to get dates but ends up finding his dream girl, Heather, is unbelievably romantic and—as far as Suhmer Zeiter and Neill Mudano are concerned—completely realistic. Two years ago, Neill took up cheerleading to hang out with Suhmer, the captain of their Bonanza High School squad in Las Vegas. "She asked me, 'Hey, why don't you come see what this cheerleading thing's all about?' This cute girl asked me," Neill says. "I couldn't say no!"

This sweet-as-*Pie* love story began in 1998 when Suhmer saw Neill dancing at a party and thought he'd be a great addition to the cheerleading squad. "I wrote him an e-mail to see if he was interested," she says. "I didn't know if he'd [join] because he was some big jock." Suhmer had an on-again, off-again relationship at the time, but she was also secretly smitten with Neill. "I did have a crush on him," she admits. Little did she know the feelings were mutual. Neill joined the cheerleading squad to get to know Suhmer better—and he also ended up getting a lot of flak from his soccer buddies. Like Oz's *Pie* posse, they didn't exactly jump for joy when he opted to play soccer and cheer in the same season. "They said I should be on the field, not the cheer squad," Neill says. But he was determined to impress Suhmer, so he worked hard on his cheering skills.

By the end of the season, Suhmer and Neill had grown close, just like the two *Pie* characters (played by Chris Klein and Mena Suvari). She'd broken up with her boyfriend, and he wasn't dating anyone, so Neill asked Suhmer to the homecoming dance. Unfortunately, her ex beat him to it. "He had asked me first," Suhmer says. "Which was the worst, because the whole [dance], I was wishing I'd gone with Neill." (Hang on to your popcorn—here comes the happy ending!) Even though Neill and Suhmer didn't arrive together, they ended up together: That night they were crowned king and queen; they went out the following evening and, says Neill, "That's the night I told her I loved her."

Suhmer and Neill are now juniors at the University of Nevada, Las Vegas, and are still going strong—not to mention big fans of *American Pie*. When Suhmer first saw the scene where Oz joins the choir, she said, "Neill, that's what you did." And Neill has no qualms about how far he went to get his girl: "Deep down I always knew she liked me from the start— and the same went for me."

Dawson's Creek

Britney Miller, 19

Andrew Goldberg, 19

LAKE OSWEGO, OREGON

"We both looked at each other and said, 'This is us—this is scary,'" says Britney Miller of the first time she and Andrew Goldberg tuned in to *Dawson's Creek* and the loves-me-loves-me-not dynamics between Joey and Dawson. "We made it a ritual that every Wednesday we would watch [the show]," Britney says. For the then—high school sophomores, following Joey (Katie Holmes) and Dawson's (James Van Der Beek) relationship was like watching their own romance unfold.

It took a while—seven years, to be exact. Although Britney and Andrew lived down the street from each other in Lake Oswego, Oregon, a small town eerily like the show's Capeside, Massachusetts, they didn't meet until the seventh grade. Andrew remembers seeing "this incredibly beautiful girl" walking down the hall. "I had to get to know her," he says, "so I invited her to my Bar Mitzvah." Britney remembers she "had no idea who he was," but her curiosity got the better of her, and she went to his party anyway. Today they bicker over whether she wore a black or a blue dress, but on that day, Andrew was just happy that Britney was willing to get to know him—and to join him on the dance floor. "Asking her to dance was one of the toughest things I remember of junior high," Andrew says, laughing. "She was two feet taller than me and absolutely made my day—made my year."

By the time they were freshmen, Britney and Andrew were inseparable. "It'd be two in the morning, and he'd come over and throw rocks at my window," says Britney. (That is *so* Joey.) She'd let him in through the back door, and they'd sneak up to her room and hang out on her bed for hours (shades of time spent in Dawson's room). Andrew even let

Britney read his scripts. (Yes, of course, he wants to be a screenwriter.) "We talked about everything," Andrew says. "There were no secrets."

Except one: Andrew was mad for Britney—who seemed to be the only one who didn't quite get it. "His friends knew, and mine were always teasing me," she says. Still, the relationship stayed platonic. "Britney always had a boyfriend," says Andrew. So three years later they each headed off to different colleges: Britney to Marymount College in Rancho Palos Verdes, California, and Andrew to George Washington University in D.C.

Following freshman year, the two went home to Lake Oswego for the summer to pick up where they'd left off—and then some. One night at Britney's, they confessed their feelings for each other and ended up dating—going to dinner and the movies—throughout the summer. "It was a few great months," says Andrew, even though the two decided not to continue the relationship long distance after they'd gone back to school. "We're pretty rational," says Britney. "We don't believe in long-distance relationships." Still the best of friends, she adds, "We're just as close as we were before—even closer." And Dawson and Joey *did* break up, you know.

star woes

love

love stories

r woes star

romance

ove

romance romance

romance

woes love s

star woes

romance
romance star wo

love lo

star woes

romance

star
WOES

Celebs may seem like they have picture-
perfect lives, but they suffer the same
romantic ups and downs that we all do.
Here, they share some of their best
and worst moments.

Who was your first crush?

Majandra Delfino *(Roswell)*

"Mine would have to be Bastian from *The Neverending Story*. The guy who played Bastian. I don't even know what his name was, but I was in love with him. I think that maybe I was in love with his character."

Vitamin C

"My first crush was a boy named Brian. I don't remember his last name. But he moved away midyear of first grade. I remember being afraid to talk to him. So I spent the first half of the year staring at him. And he left. Up and left. And we had a party for him to say good-bye, and I finally went up to him and said, 'Good-bye.' And that was the only thing I ever said to him. So from that moment on, I've acted upon my crushes."

Brendan Fehr (Roswell)

"My biggest celebrity crush was Reese Witherspoon. *Freeway* did it for me. Now she's married to Ryan Phillipe, so I've got to move on to someone else. But it was Reese for a very long time."

Seth Green (Buffy the Vampire Slayer)

"I was literally in, like, first grade, and there was this girl in my class, and my grandma was working at this hotel where they put chocolates on people's beds. So she got me a big fat box of chocolates, and I trudged over to this girl's house in the snow and gave it to her on Valentine's Day. I sat there on her couch while she ate them and then she kicked me out."

Charlie O'Connell *(Dude, Where's My Car?)*

"Yes. My brother [Jerry] picks the worst blind dates I go on. I've done it for him and he's done it for me. But it's great when you go on one and by the end of the night you are completely good friends."

What's the craziest thing you've done for love?

Mike Piazza (New York Mets)

"Craziest? Probably buying her something really expensive. There was this one girl who I bought a ton of flowers for one day. Like, her whole office, I filled it with flowers. When she came in, you couldn't even see anything. That was fun. It went pretty well."

What was your most embarrassing dating moment?

Erika Christensen *(Traffic)*

"On a date when I was really young, like thirteen, I was walking with a guy and he put out his hand so we could hold hands while we were walking. At first I shook his hand and he was, like, 'No, no, no.' Then I gave him five and he's like, 'No, no, no.' Then I finally realized what he meant, and was, like, 'Oh no!'"

Tom Dumont (guitarist, No Doubt)

"It was my first date with my girlfriend. I had never been to her house before, so I walked up to the wrong one! This really tough guy answered the door. Meanwhile, she was next door, watching me go to the wrong house!"

Christopher Gorham *(Popular)*

"My senior prom, I got food poisoning. So I spent the entire night in the bathroom. It was not romantic at all. I didn't have a girlfriend, so a friend of mine at the last minute asked me, 'You wanna go, just as friends?' So I said, 'All right.' It was my senior prom. I had to go.

"We went out to dinner. I ordered calamari for the first time and proceeded to get intensely sick. I literally spent the entire dance in the bathroom. I'd come out, and immediately have to go back to the rest room. I barely got her home in time and got back to my house before my tuxedo was soiled beyond belief."

Gabrielle Reese (professional volleyball player)

"I really liked this boy when I was, like, sixteen. He was very cute, and we went on a date to the movies and I had on a new outfit. It was a pink skirt with a powder blue and pink top. I got my period in the movie theater and didn't realize it. Sometimes you sit on the seat and it's hot! Anyway, I didn't realize it but, he was a gentleman. He took his sweater and tied it around my waist. We walked out last, and he took me home. I changed before we went back out. That was pretty mortifying."

Gabrielle Union (Bring It On)

"My most embarrassing moment was with my ex-boyfriend, who is now an NBA all-star. He broke up with me in front of my parents at a basketball game. That's humiliating and embarrassing all wrapped into one."

Beverley Mitchell (7th Heaven)

"It was sophomore year. I was all excited because there was a big school dance. I was talking to this guy I liked, and my friend—trying to do me a favor—told me I should pull my pants down a little because they were too high. She ended up 'pants-ing' me in front of the guy I liked and our entire school. I ran off, thinking, How can I face them? It's a joke now [giving my pants] a little tug."

first kiss

holding hands

dreamy

romance

romance

love

roman

love stories

trendspotters
ROMANCE

We asked the *Teen People* Trendspotters,
a group of more than ten thousand readers
ages thirteen to twenty-one, to share their stories of
true romance. Here's what they said!

On Embarrassing Dates

"I was to meet my friend Ben and his friends at our semiformal dance. My friend Brandy was going with Ben and I was going with his friend, so for me it was a blind date! Brandy and I got all dazzled up and were at the dance about five minutes before Ben and my blind date were supposed to show up. I was so nervous, I kept asking Brandy how

I looked and if she thought he would like me. (She knew the guy through Ben.) She said that she thought he would and that I shouldn't be nervous. So I kind of calmed down a little. I mean, it wasn't like I was going to marry the guy. Finally Ben arrived. Brandy and I were already on the dance floor, so he came up and said hello and then motioned for his friend to come over to us. As he was introducing me to him, his friend and I started laughing hysterically. It turned out that his friend, my blind date, was my cousin Matt! We had a great time at the dance and laughed about it all night. We still laugh about it!" —*Jessica*

* * *

"I'd been dating this guy, Jeremy, since fourth grade. We were little childhood sweethearts, and we went out, on and off, up until ninth grade. At the end of our seventh-grade year, he dumped me and I was so upset. I pined away for him all summer, even though he had another girlfriend. I swore that I would get him back before eighth grade started.

"We were both invited to this pool party. Everyone was going except Jeremy's new girlfriend. I'd been in Georgia, and he hadn't seen me all summer. I decided that I had to show up looking awesome.

"I never wear two-pieces, but I went out and bought a pretty blue bikini to wear. I showed up looking great, all made-up, and really tan. I flashed him my best movie-star smile a couple of times, and batted my eyelashes and laughed at his jokes. It was all going great when we decided that we were going to play volleyball for a while.

"The girls all ran into the dressing room, and those who had been swimming started changing into shorts and tanks or slipping them over their swimsuits. My top was dry, so I put a shirt on over it, but my bottoms were wet, so I changed into underwear and shorts.

"We played volleyball for a while, but we wanted to go swimming again, so everyone went back into the locker room. I had to hit the ladies' room, so the girls were already back in the pool when I came back to the locker room. I ran as fast as I could back to the pool area, not wanting to miss anything. When Jeremy saw me enter the pool area, he got out of the pool and walked over to me. Yes! My big chance to look cool to him. We started talking, and, as we did, I ripped off my shirt, revealing my bikini top. He was smiling and talking, and I was laughing. Everything was perfect. I unbuttoned my shorts and slipped them off to reveal my . . .

underwear! I'd forgotten to change back into my bikini bottoms. He didn't laugh right away because he looked confused, as if he couldn't figure out if I'd changed bathing suits. But this tall man from across the pool yelled, 'Honey in her drawers!' And the entire party looked at me. The laughter from them and from Jeremy was uncontrollable! I stood there, frozen in my underwear, in front of my ex-boyfriend, not knowing that he would ask me out again a week later." —*Meredith*

On First Kisses

"The first time I kissed my boyfriend we were at the skating rink. His cousin and my cousin were hanging out together also. So at the end of the session, we (both couples) were up against the wall kissing and dead to the world. When my boyfriend and I were done kissing, I opened my eyes to see my aunt standing there in front of me with her hands on her hips. She told my mom, and I was grounded from skating for four months. That didn't stop my boyfriend from coming to the house, though (hee hee)." —*Marjorie*

* * *

"I have an unbelievable kiss story for you. I met a friend of a friend, and we started e-mailing each other and being really flirty, so we decided to have a double date with our best friends. It was really cold and snowy, so we decided to go skiing. I had never been skiing before, but he had, so he was showing me the ropes. After a few trial runs down the hills (and falling on my butt), he decided to take me on the ski lift to go on some more ski adventures. It was so cold, my teeth started chattering, so he put his arm around me and pulled me closer to him. Both of our skis were just dangling in the air, and I was telling him how amazing it was being on the ski lift. He said, 'It's not half as amazing as being up here with you.' With that, he leaned in and kissed. I remember feeling his ice-cold nose. It was a kiss I'll never forget!" —*Danielle*

✳ ✳ ✳

"I don't want to give out my guy's name, so I'll call him his nickname from me: Mr. Bigglesworth! Mr. Bigglesworth was 'that guy who sits next to me all the time in English' for the longest time. I liked him a lot at first, but not in the romantic sense. Though he was gorgeous, he was never serious. He was the class clown, and what kind of boyfriend is that? I was being completely dense and never really thought about why this incredibly awesome guy kept sitting at the double desk where I always sat so it was just the two of us! After a while, I decided he would make a great friend, if not more than that. We got to be friends and we exchanged e-mail addresses.

"Well, the barrage of jokes we sent back and forth turned from quick notes and party invites to deep conversations and debates one-on-one. Then I began thinking . . . Wow! This is a really great guy! We have so much in common, and he's so cute. I was officially crushing!

"One day, he asked for my phone number for class assignments and homework help, of course. I immediately scrawled my number on his palm, and he called that afternoon. We chatted for a few minutes about our classes together (we had history together and I didn't even know it!), but then he started asking me questions about what he should do about a girl he knew. He told me how she had the most beautiful eyes, long, shiny hair, a dazzling smile and a great personality to boot! As I was counseling him on his romantic life, I was imagining this girl . . . the perfect girl, everything I wasn't. I was getting a little depressed, and the conversation finally ended. I hung up and sighed out loud, wondering how I was ever going to get over this perfect guy.

"I went to school the next day and was moping around. It was completely obvious I wasn't my normally bubbly, peppy, outgoing self. All my friends were worried, but I insisted nothing was wrong, and the questions stopped coming. Mr. Bigglesworth was in my next class then, English.

"I walked into the classroom and made a weak attempt at my usual grin. A look of concern crossed Mr. Bigglesworth's face, but he didn't say anything out of the ordinary, so I convinced myself he didn't notice. I sat down in my usual spot next to him, and asked the one question I had been anticipating and dreading all day. I asked how it went with his crush. He looked at me, and those stunning green eyes suddenly became so serious, I didn't know what to think.

"I looked at him curiously, a joke forming in my mind, when he answered in a very deep, serious, sexy voice. (I'll never forget exactly what he said next!) 'I haven't asked her yet . . . I'm afraid I'll lose the friendship of the greatest girl I've ever known. The smartest, funniest, most beautiful woman in the world. If I had the guts, I'd tell her all this and ask her if she'd be mine.'

"I looked at him blankly, and suddenly it clicked! He was talking about me! I think my eyes must have widened to nothing but pupils, because he smiled that killer grin of his and asked the easiest question I've ever had to answer. 'So, Alexis Leigh . . . is that a yes?' Obviously it was, and he leaned over and kissed me right there. We're still together today, and going strong!" —*Alexis*

* * *

"My first kiss was when I was in seventh grade. . . . I was so nervous and totally thought I was going to spaz. I liked this kid for a while and he was perfect and I didn't want to screw up. So all my friends and I went to the movies, and he and I sat next to each other. I waited practically until the movie was almost over for him to make the first move. Then, finally, he threw his arms around me really fast and started to kiss me. At the pace he was going, it was like he was in a race. I swear to God it felt like someone was having a seizure inside my mouth. It was so gross. That had to be the worst kiss ever; too bad for him that he lost the race!" —*Noel*

* * *

"I have a great unusual first-kiss experience! It was with my first boyfriend in sixth grade, right after the Valentine's Day dance. All during the dance, my friends and his friends wanted us to kiss, but neither of us wanted to do it in front of every-one. So after the dance, he went and got my jacket and then we went outside. My best friend and his best friend were also with us. Well, when we got outside, we went behind a tree, but of course, our two friends could still see us. It was really awkward, and then all of a sudden I actually counted! I went, 'One, two, three,' and we kissed! Now when I look back on it, I feel like such a loser, but hey, it was my first kiss and I will always remember it!" —*Lauren*

On True Romance

"A few summers ago I met the guy of my life. He was all-around perfect. The twist . . . I met him on vacation. He lives in North Carolina, and I live in New Mexico. Anyway, we had a blast together that summer, but eventually I had to go home. The last night I was there we said our good-byes and promised to write and call, but I was almost positive I would never see him again. Well, that night I went to bed with tears in my eyes, but the next morning was a different story. I woke up with my family telling me I had a visitor, and guess who it was? My dream guy! He told me he needed to see me again and took me out to breakfast to have one last day together. I almost melted when he did this and I will never forget it, either." —*Emily*

✳ ✳ ✳

"Okay . . . I think I have one of the craziest romance stories. . . . Remember in sixth grade or so when your class got pen pals? Well, I got a boy named Bryan, who lived in Florida. I was excited just to write letters to someone that far away. I finally got my first letter from him. It was in all different colors (pink, purple, etc.), with little happy faces drawn all over it and stuff. I still have it to this day.

"We continued to write even after the class project was over. We exchanged letters at least every other week for years. He was my friend, too. If I was having a bad day, I would just write it all down and send the letter to him. Then, in my sophomore year in high school, we started calling each other on the phone. I realized how awesome he was, but he was too far away to think of anything else happening.

"Last summer I took a vacation in Europe, but halfway through it I had to fly to Florida for a photo shoot for an athletic award. The only problem was that I was going to have to fly in a couple of days early and I had nowhere to stay. I called Bryan, and his family said no problem, I could stay over with them. I was excited; actually, we both were.

"I tried not to think about it, but I ended up psyching myself out thinking things like, What if his family can't stand me; what if he can't stand me? Then, on the plane ride to finally meet him, I lost my luggage, so the first time I saw him, when I got off the plane, I was all teary-eyed. But there he was, standing there with a rose for me, making sure everything was okay.

"Immediately I knew how truly special he was.

"The first night I was there we stayed up all night talking about life and such and we both realized that we were falling even deeper for each other. Then the second night, we were lying on the bed looking at old letters I had written him and he leaned over and kissed me . . . the greatest kiss of my entire life.

"Now I am back here in California going to Cal State Long Beach, and he's in Florida going to college. We talk all the time now about us . . . about trips we would like to take (he's never been to California). That was the greatest summer, and now he's my best friend . . . if only a whole country didn't separate us!" —*Erin*

✳ ✳ ✳

"My story begins when I was in eighth grade. My best friend introduced me to a guy who I ended up having a big crush on. In my part of the country, a lot of people don't make it all the way through high school, so when you finish middle school, you have a graduation and a prom. Well, the guy asked me to go to the prom with him, so I said yes. We went and we ended up having a really great time. We kept in contact over the summer, and he's one of my really good friends now, but he told me a big secret about himself that he found out this summer. He told me that he was gay. I was crushed, but supportive. I've been supportive of him and his new boyfriend, even when the majority of my friends weren't." —Amy

If you have enjoyed *Love Stories* then we're sure you'll like receiving *Teen People* magazine every month!

· Go on tour with your favorite bands!

· Visit the sets of top TV shows!

· Meet real-life teens doing really cool things!

· See candid shots of the top celebs at work and play!

· Get the real scoop on dating, school, drugs, love and more!

· Keep up-to-date with the must-have CDs!

If you'd like a *FREE PREVIEW ISSUE* please call 800-284-0200 or go to our website at www.teenpeople.com

TEENS....TEACHERS....PARENTS

Celebrate teens and their achievements!
Do you know a teenager who has made a difference?

Teens today are affecting the world more than at any other time in history. *Teen People®* magazine and HarperCollins Publishers want to celebrate teens making a positive difference in their communities and in our world. Introducing the

TEEN PEOPLE COMMUNITY ACTION AWARDS

Any teen age 13 to 21 who has made a significant contribution to the community is eligible. No act of kindness is too small, no plan too grand. It could take place at school, home or the local hangout. It can be an act of courage or kindness. If a teen you know has touched one heart, or one hundred hearts, we want to know about it.

What to do: In 500 words or less, tell us about the teen who inspires you. Tell us about your community and how this amazing teenager has made it a better place to live. Send your essay, along with the family contact information of the teen to *TEEN PEOPLE* COMMUNITY ACTION AWARD, HarperCollins Children's Books, **1350 Avenue of the Americas, New York, NY 10019.**

The Award: The teen whose story is the most inspiring and impressive to our distinguished panel of judges will win a $2,500 scholarship, a trip to the star-studded *TEEN PEOPLE* COMMUNITY ACTION AWARD Ceremony in New York or Los Angeles in September 2002, a 2-year subscription to *Teen People* magazine, and a selection of books from HarperCollins Publishers. In addition, the winner's name will be announced in an issue of *Teen People*.

Three 1st Prize winners will each receive a $500 scholarship, a trip to the awards ceremony in September 2002, a 1-year subscription to *Teen People* magazine, and a selection of books from HarperCollins Publishers.